W9-CZK-895

Amanda Bynes

Amie Jane Leavitt

P.O. Box 196
Hockessin, Delaware 19707
Visit us on the web: www.mitchelllane.com
Comments? email us: mitchelllane@mitchelllane.com

Mitchell Lane PUBLISHERS

Printing   1   2   3   4   5   6   7   8   9

A Robbie Reader
Contemporary Biography/Science Biography

Albert Einstein	Albert Pujols	Alex Rodriguez
Aly and AJ	**Amanda Bynes**	Brittany Murphy
Charles Schulz	Dakota Fanning	Dale Earnhardt Jr.
Donovan McNabb	Drake Bell & Josh Peck	Dr. Seuss
Dylan & Cole Sprouse	Henry Ford	Hilary Duff
Jamie Lynn Spears	Jessie McCartney	Johnny Gruelle
LeBron James	Mandy Moore	Mia Hamm
Miley Cyrus	Philo T. Farnsworth	Raven Symone
Robert Goddard	Shaquille O'Neal	The Story of Harley-Davidson
Syd Hoff	Tiki Barber	Thomas Edison
Tony Hawk		

Library of Congress Cataloging-in-Publication Data
Leavitt, Amie Jane.
    Amanda Bynes / by Amie Jane Leavitt.
      p. cm.
    "A Robbie Reader."
    Includes bibliographical references and index.
    ISBN-13: 978-1-58415-594-2 (library bound)
    1. Bynes, Amanda, 1986—Juvenile literature. 2. Actors—United States—Biography—Juvenile literature. I. Title.
PN2287.B94L43 2008
792.02'8092—dc22
[B]   2007000800

ABOUT THE AUTHOR: Amie Jane Leavitt is the author of numerous books, articles, puzzles, workbooks, and tests for kids and teens. Ms. Leavitt is a former teacher who has taught all subjects and grade levels. She loves to travel, play tennis, and learn new things every day as she writes. Like Amanda Bynes, she, too, believes in following her dreams.

PHOTO CREDITS: Cover—Peter Kramer/Getty Images; p. 4—James Devaney/WireImage; p. 6—ALLSTAR/Globe Photos; p. 7—Dimitrios Kambouris/WireImage; p. 8—Clinton H. Wallace/IPOL/Globe Photos; p. 10—Steve Granitz Archive/WireImage; p. 12—Kevin Winter/Getty Images; p. 15—Scott Humbert/Warner Bros./Getty Images; p. 16—Andrea Renault/Globe Photos; p. 22—Ken Babolcsay/IPOL/Globe Photos; p. 24—Jeff Vespa/WireImage; p. 25—Stephen Shugerman/Getty Images; p. 27—Vince Bucci/Getty Images.

TABLE OF CONTENTS

Amanda does a little dance on the stage of MTV's *Total Request Live.*
She has been performing onstage since before she was ten.

The Laugh Factory

Young Amanda Bynes walked onto the stage. She was at the Laugh Factory in Los Angeles. This was a very famous place. Many **comedians** (kuh-MEE-dee-uhns) had performed here. Amanda's job that night was to make people laugh. She was a little nervous, but also excited. She hoped that people would think she was funny, even though she was so young. Amanda was only ten years old. Most of the other performers were grown-ups.

Amanda did a great job. The **audience** (AW-dee-enss) loved her. They laughed at her jokes. They clapped when she did something silly onstage. Amanda was very happy with her performance. She thought it was fun being a comedian. She enjoyed making people laugh.

Amanda gives two thumbs up to her fans at the 17th Nickelodeon Kids'
Choice Awards.

Although Amanda believes she is a normal teen, her fans know she has special talents as a comedian and actress.

One night, an important person came to see Amanda perform. His name was Dan Schneider (SHNEYE-der). He worked for Nickelodeon (nik-uh-LOW-dee-uhn). He thought Amanda was funny. He wanted her to perform on television. Amanda was very excited about the chance to be a television **actress** (AK-tres). She told Mr. Schneider she would take the job.

Amanda poses for the camera with Rick and Lynn Bynes, her parents. Her father is a part-time comedian.

Like Father, Like Daughter

Amanda Laura Bynes was born on April 3, 1986, in Thousand Oaks, California. Her dad, Richard Bynes, is a dentist. Her mom, Lynn Organ Bynes, is a dental assistant. Amanda is their third child. She has an older brother named Tommy and an older sister named Jillian. One of Amanda's parents is Catholic and the other is Jewish. Amanda considers herself to be Jewish.

Amanda has always liked to tell jokes and make people laugh. In this way, she is like her father. Richard Bynes fixes people's teeth during the day. At night, he sometimes performs onstage as a comedian.

When Amanda was thirteen, she attended the YoungStar Awards at Universal Studios.

Longtime actor and comedian Richard Pryor inspired Amanda by teaching her how to improve her comedy act. Pryor passed away on December 10, 2006, at the age of sixty-five.

Amanda wanted to make people laugh too. She dreamed about being an actress and a comedian someday.

When Amanda was only seven years old, her dreams came true. Her first acting job was on a television **commercial** (kuh-MER-shul). It was for Nestlé's Buncha Crunch candies. She really liked this job because she could eat a lot of chocolate while she worked.

Later, Amanda started going to a comedy camp during the summertime. She took lessons on how to become a better comedian. Her teachers were famous comedians like Richard Pryor (PREYE-er) and Arsenio (ar-SIH-nee-oh) Hall. She learned a lot from them.

11

Amanda thanks her fans for voting for her show to win a 2004 Kids' Choice Award.

CHAPTER THREE

Television Years

Soon, Amanda was performing onstage. Her first performances were at the Comedy Store in Los Angeles. Later, she performed at the Laugh Factory. Performing at both of these places helped Amanda become a better actress.

Amanda's first job for Nickelodeon was on the television show called *All That*. She performed on this show from 1996 until 1999. Many kids liked watching the show. It was filled with short skits, music, and **impersonations** (im-per-suh-NAY-shuns) of famous people. Amanda was one of the most popular performers on the show. Nickelodeon knew this, and in 1999 they asked her to be the star

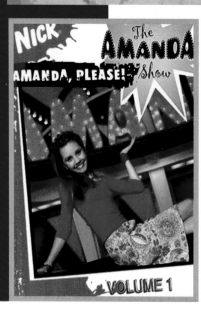

Fans loved *The Amanda Show,* which ran from 1999 through 2002. At age thirteen, Amanda was the youngest star to be given her own variety show.

of her own **variety show** (vah-REYE-eh-tee show). She was the youngest person to ever do this. Her show was called *The Amanda Show.*

This show was similar to *All That.* Amanda got to play many different parts. She really liked playing the part of Penelope (puh-NEH-luh-pee) Taynt. This was a crazy fan who really wanted to meet Amanda. She thought it was funny to play the part of someone who liked her so much! *The Amanda Show* was on television for three years. Kids liked this show so much that they voted Amanda as their favorite actress in the Kids' Choice Awards several times.

Amanda (left) and Jennie Garth play two sisters on the show *What I Like About You.* The show ran from 2002 to 2006.

In 2002, when she was sixteen, Amanda became an actress on the WB. This television network broadcasts shows that are mainly for teens. Amanda played the part of Holly Tyler on the show *What I Like About You.* She costarred with Jennie Garth, who had become famous during the 1990s. She was on a television show called *Beverly Hills, 90210.* Amanda and Jennie played sisters on *What I Like About You.*

Amanda signs a movie poster for *What a Girl Wants*. For this film, she spent most of her time on location in London, England.

On the Big Screen

Amanda liked performing on television, but she wanted to try out different things. She thought that maybe she'd like to be in movies too. Her first movie was in 2002 with Frankie Muniz (MYOO-niz). He was the star from the television show *Malcolm in the Middle*. Their movie was called *Big Fat Liar*. Amanda played Frankie's best friend in the movie. It was a very popular movie for kids.

Amanda's next big movie was called *What a Girl Wants*. This movie was filmed in London, England. Amanda had never been there before. She loved learning more about the city while she filmed the movie. She enjoyed working with the other famous actors on the set. She

Amanda and Frankie Muniz stroll through a scene for the 2002 movie *Big Fat Liar*.

also liked wearing the pretty ball gown at the end of the movie.

This was Amanda's first leading role in a movie. That meant that she had the main part. She played a girl named Daphne (DAF-nee) Reynolds. Daphne lives in New York City. Her father lives in England, but she has never met him. She decides to travel all the way to

Amanda (right) had to pretend she was a boy in the movie *She's the Man*. She had to wear a wig and a suit and even make her voice sound like a boy!

England to go see him. Amanda did such a great job in the movie that she got another Kids' Choice Award for favorite actress.

Amanda's movie career didn't stop there. In 2005, she filmed the movie *Lovewrecked.* Her next film, *She's the Man,* was released in 2006. In this movie, her character dresses up like a boy so she can prove her skills on the

19

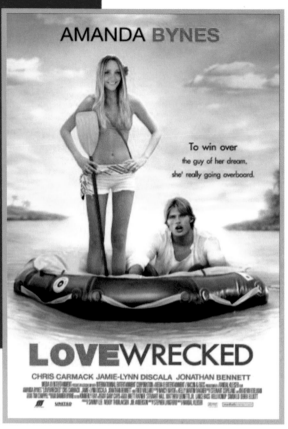

Amanda gets shipwrecked with her music idol in the movie *Lovewrecked*.

soccer field. In summer 2007, she played Penny Pingleton in the star-studded movie *Hairspray*.

Amanda wants to keep performing in movies, but she is very careful about the movies she chooses. She likes movies that have messages. She likes to feel that she is a better person after she sees a movie, so these are the only kinds of movies that she wants to make.

Amanda plays Penny Pingleton, and Zac Efron (left) plays Link Larkin in the 2007 remake of *Hairspray*. Also in the cast are many other well-known actors, including John Travolta, Michelle Pfeiffer, Christopher Walken, and Queen Latifah.

Amanda is featured on the *Today Show* as she helps build a house for Habitat for Humanity. She has always enjoyed helping others.

Just Like Other Teens

Many people wonder what famous people are like in real life. Amanda is just like most other teens. She likes to live a normal life. She loves hanging out with her friends and driving her car. She wants to go to college someday.

Amanda has several hobbies, including drawing. She likes to draw fashion pictures. At one time, she wanted to design clothes. Amanda also likes to paint. Once she painted a picture of David Letterman. She gave it to him when she was a guest on his program, *Late Show with David Letterman*. Amanda also enjoys writing. She writes in her diary as often as she can. She even puts some of her entries on her web site so that her fans can read them.

In 2003, Amanda participated in a fashion show and luncheon to raise money for the Caring for Children and Families with AIDS program.

Amanda likes to do things for other people. "It's really a fulfilling feeling when you know you've helped somebody," Amanda said in 2005. Amanda started volunteering when she was a kid. She believes this is a good thing for all kids to do. "If you start young, you'll always have a love for it," she says.

Over the years, Amanda has volunteered at homeless shelters. She has helped build

Amanda and Jillian are not only sisters, they are also best friends.

houses for Habitat for Humanity. She has cleaned parks, helped raise money for animal rescue, and visited sick children in hospitals.

Amanda likes to volunteer with her friends and family. Sometimes she'll spend her holidays serving others.

Amanda is very close to her family. Her best friend is her older sister. She is glad that her parents have helped her follow her dreams. She is also glad that they have helped her make good decisions.

"I love them because they accept me for who I am," Amanda says about her parents, "and they love me with all my faults. I am so grateful for them. I want to be with them forever. This is a good time to tell you! I'm never leaving!"

Some famous people do not like it when people ask them for **autographs** (AW-toh-grafs). Not Amanda. She loves her fans. She is glad that they like her performances.

Sometimes Amanda is compared to other famous people her age. She doesn't like that.

Amanda loves signing autographs for her fans. Here she meets and greets some of her fans at the 5th Annual Family Television Awards.

She thinks that people should be themselves. She doesn't believe that she is better or worse than anyone else. She has just tried to follow her dreams. And she thinks everyone else should do the same.

Amanda hopes to keep acting and making people laugh. If her fans are lucky, she'll get to do just that!

CHRONOLOGY

1986   Amanda Laura Bynes is born in Thousand Oaks, California, on April 3.

1993   Amanda is in her first television commercial.

1996–1999 She is in the Nickelodeon series *All That.*

1999–2002 She hosts her own show, *The Amanda Show.*

2002   She plays Kaylee in *Big Fat Liar* with Frankie Muniz.

2002–2006 She plays Holly Tyler in the TV comedy series *What I Like About You.*

2003   Amanda has the starring role of Daphne Reynolds in *What a Girl Wants.*

2004   She graduates from Thousand Oaks High School after taking an independent study program.

2005   She is the voice of Piper in *Robots,* and also plays Jenny Riley in *Lovewrecked.*

2006   She plays Viola Hastings in *She's the Man. Lovewrecked* is shown in theaters.

2007   *Hairspray,* in which Amanda plays Penny Pingleton, opens in theaters.

FILMOGRAPHY

2002 *Big Fat Liar*

2003 *What a Girl Wants*

2005 *Lovewrecked*

2006 *She's the Man*

2007 *Hairspray*

FIND OUT MORE

Articles

Baer, Deborah. "Amanda Bynes is MISS INDEPENDENT." *Cosmo Girl*. October 2005, pp. 110–113.

Barker, Lynn. "Amanda Bynes: Tea and Scones, Anyone?" *Teen Hollywood*. April 3, 2003.

Bryson, Jodi Lynn. "Hangin' With." *Girls' Life*. October 2002, p. 54.

"Entertainment Review." *Teen People*. October 2002, p. 90.

Feder-Feitel, Lisa. "Amazing Amanda." *Scholastic Scope*. April 10, 2006, p. 18.

Laufer-Krebs, Bonnie. "Amanda Bynes—A Girl Who Knows What She Wants." *Kids Tribute*. Spring 2003, p. 31.

FIND OUT MORE

Works Consulted

"Amanda Bynes." *People*. March 27, 2006, p. 85.

Hicks, Tameka L. "Amanda Bynes on Volunteering."
USA Weekend Magazine. April 24, 2005.

"It Genuine." *Entertainment Weekly*. June 28, 2002,
p. 69.

Koehler, Robert. "Man Gives Bard a Contempo Kick."
Entertainment Review. March 13, 2006, pp. 35–
42.

Lyon, Shauna. "She's the Man." *New Yorker*. April 10,
2006, p. 18.

Noh, David. "She's the Man." *Film Journal
International*. May 2006, pp. 52–53.

Tomlinson, Sarah. "A Screen Everygirl Stretches Her
Skills." *The Boston Globe*. March 12, 2006.

Wethington, Jessica. "Amanda Bynes." *Daily Variety*.
November 1, 2000, p. A7.

On the Internet

The Official Amanda Bynes Web Site
http://www.amandabynes.com
ELLEgirl: "She's All That"
http://www.ellegirl.com/article/
article.do?articleid=5024

actress (AK-tres)—a woman who performs in a play, television show, or movie.

audience (AW-dee-enss)—people who watch a play or show.

autographs (AW-toh-grafs)—signatures from famous people.

comedians (kuh-MEE-dee-uns)—people who tell jokes and make other people laugh.

commercial (kuh-MER-shul)—an advertisement on the television.

impersonation (im-per-suh-NAY-shun)—an act in which a person talks, walks, and acts like someone else.

variety show (vah-REYE-eh-tee show)—a program that features different acts, such as a funny short play, comedians, and singers.

INDEX